GETTING THE MOST FROM PARTNERSHIPS

WITH THOSE CUSTOMERS WHICH

MEAN THE MOST TO YOUR COMPANY

Purposeful
Selling

George E. Devitt

"ALL CUSTOMERS ARE EQUAL, BUT SOME
CUSTOMERS ARE MORE EQUAL THAN OTHERS."

Purposeful Selling

To Leslie, without whom my life would be far less rich and who is the person that I know God intended for me to be with forever.

Table of Contents

Foreword

This book is an attempt to condense over thirty years of sales, sales management and sales training in the space provided between its front and back covers. The author has attempted to document, in written form, the "best practices" that he has observed and put into practice while selling to what are variously known as key accounts, strategic accounts, global accounts, major accounts or some similar categorization or stratification which represents the significance of these customers to the company for whom the sales professional works. Those who will benefit the most from this book are the sales professionals who sell to customers which have a *material impact* upon their employer's (their company's) top line, bottom line or both. Its greatest benefits will accrue to the sales professional or sales manager who is engaged predominantly in Business-to-Business selling. Moreover, the type of B-to-B sales professional for whom this book will be most beneficial are those whose sales, or "deals," are typically characterized by their large-dollar-amount, their long sales cycle, the complexity of the customer's buying process, the number of individuals within the customer's organization which are typically involved in the "buying decision," and will most often be characterized by multi-year contractual commitments. Not all of these characteristics need to be present for the principles described herein to be beneficial, but at least one or more should be.

Those engaged in the "transactional sale" may find some benefit in reading this book, as it will benefit them in that they will "up their game" and enhance the degree of sales professionalism which will separate them from their competitors. "Transactional sales" are those sales which are likely to enjoy the benefit of the "one-call-close." While the products sold in a "transactional sale" need not be commodities, many of the characteristics of commodity selling may be present. For example, customers which are engaged in a "transactional" buying decision will often place a high degree of importance on factors such as price, delivery, and terms and conditions. They are not likely to place a great deal of emphasis on "value-added" services or product features and functionality.

How does a salesperson make the transition to "sales professional," and then to a "Consultative Sales Professional" and ultimately to a "Trusted Advisor" to his or her customer or client? The author's premise is that first, the individual must make the transition in his or her own mind that he or she has chosen to make sales "a profession." And that it is, indeed, an honorable profession. As with any profession, the investment in one's continuing development is required: staying abreast of market trends, product innovations, increasing his knowledge base, honing her skill set, and 'putting himself in the shoes of his customer.'

While she is an "advocate" for her customer, this sales professional is always mindful of where those bi-weekly paychecks come from! The customer or client certainly knows – and yet, many a sales professional has been known to "cross the line?" Instead, we must be always mindful that our relationship with our customer is not a "win-lose" proposition, but an opportunity for both organizations to "win." And to accomplish that goal requires that the client looks to his sales representative not just as "the face of his vendor," but as a "Trusted Advisor" who is always seeking ways to improve the client's business by identifying sources of new revenue or opportunities to reduce costs. *Purposeful Selling*™ is a framework for operating in this rarified environment, resulting in the sales professional taking pride in his or her "Profession" and the customer or client attributing significant "value" to the role of the Sales Professional with whom he or she has the opportunity and "privilege" to work.

There are three guiding principles associated with what we refer to as *Purposeful Selling*™. The reader should be prepared to be "underwhelmed," as he or she will see that all three principles are obvious, common sense and basic, and for most, even intuitive. And yet, a rigorous self-inspection and analysis of the day-to-day activities of the sales professional will almost always result in the conclusion that these most obvious and basic of principles are rarely put into practice with any consistency or discipline. The three simple principles which form the foundation for *Purposeful Selling*™ are:

- That customers buy from suppliers not because of how much <u>they</u> know about our products or services, but about how much <u>we know</u> about their business and our ability to solve their business problems;
- That these types of sales are made top – down, but that the preparation for the top-down selling is done from the bottom – up;
- And that a formal presentation to the ultimate decision maker is not a "backup" strategy, but is fundamental to success in establishing long-term partnerships with our customers.

There are no surprises in any of these principles. As noted, they are obvious and even intuitive to almost every experienced sales professional. But in over three decades of observing sales professionals in their day-to-day activities, very few of them "walk the talk" and practice these principles.

This book will attempt to "unpack" each of these principles and the many nuances associated with each. The author has made every effort for this book to be a practical guide and not a lengthy discussion of sales theories, buyer personas or the latest "sales techniques." While there may be a benefit to comparing and contrasting "The Ben Franklin Close" with the "Puppy Dog Close," the reader will not find topics of this sort contained herein.

The reader will also notice that the author tends to avoid references to "sales rep," "salesman," or "salesperson. The avoidance of these terms, and using the alternative phraseology of "sales professional" is quite intentional. If we are enhancing the stature of selling to that of a "profession," the author believes that nomenclature and terminology are important. Just as a CPA would recoil at being called a "bookkeeper," it is our hope that those engaged in the *profession* of selling would also use terminology commensurate with the significance of the role he or she is filling. While every role within almost any company is important, "sales" is in a unique category.

Companies don't typically go out of business because the person responsible for developing product documentation fouled up.

But when a *post-mortem* is conducted of those companies which have the misfortune of going out of business, it's almost always due to a lack of sales. A sale is what provides the fuel necessary for a company to operate. Without a sale, the need for an assembly technician on the manufacturing line, or for an Accounts Receivable clerk, or for the company's Controller – the need for any of these people or for the function which they perform goes away.

But as with any such topic, one must have a "balanced" view. Indeed, we are summarily opposed to the practice of some companies in which their sales organizations are treated as *prima donnas*. By way of example, the best sales professional in the world cannot overcome the reputation for shoddy workmanship which a company will get by failing to place an adequate emphasis on the quality of its products or services.

And thus, it is with these recognitions in mind that the benefits which will result from the practice of *Purposeful Selling*™ are successful.

Wherever possible, real-life examples are used to illustrate these principles as they are put into practice. Customer names, for obvious reasons, are fictional – but the examples and case studies are not. The mastery and practice of the disciplines described will raise the level of professionalism of any sales professional, sales manager or sales executive, and <u>will</u> lead to lasting, mutually beneficial partnerships with your customers.

It Takes a Team
<u>Chapter 1</u>

There is no "I" in "sales." While this book makes frequent reference to "the sales professional," it should be noted at the outset that sales is a team sport. While some sales professionals can play many roles – in general, it's important to note that when selling to key accounts it is necessary to have a team of people who can play different roles and who have different skill sets.

But the obsession with finding the "super star" salesperson is understandable. Who doesn't want to employ a rock star? A great deal of time and energy is often spent in an effort to find the person with the perfect combination of verve, rapport, professionalism, discipline and other sales skills, <u>as well as</u> the technical skills required to support a complex and sophisticated product or system. But such efforts are misguided. Even if the perfect person exists, more than one "superstar" sales professional is needed to win and retain major accounts.

In the hiring process, many companies over-emphasize the importance associated with a salesperson's qualifications, experience and achievements. It is generally not the individual sales professional, but rather the sales *team* that is the key to landing and <u>retaining</u> such key account sales. Teamwork is the only time-tested manner of sustaining an enduring and mutually successful relationship.

In turn, team performance is influenced by the types of which it is comprised, and not all of these are sales professionals. Certain combinations of personality types and job functions perform better than others.

When the thinking shifts from *player* to *team*, the responsibility for performance is shared across all team members.

It becomes the responsibility of the Sales Manager to figure out what the proper balance of skills is necessary – and this balance of skills is not likely to be found in one person, but several. A quick list might include:

1. **The Opener**. This person is a rapport builder. Someone who can generate interest,

open the door and secure a meeting with an executive sponsor.

2. **The Technician**. A person who demonstrates that you "know your stuff." This is your industry expert, who can provide the necessary language, history and context to the discussion as it relates to the prospect's company and its potential purchase from your company.

3. **The Flow Monitor.** This is a very important relationship person. He or she gets a sense of the prospect's people and keeps the sales dialogue moving. This person is a facilitator more than a sales driver. We've all observed people who do this well. They're the types who may remain silent during most of a meeting, but who can detect when the direction of the meeting is headed the wrong way – and can avert a potential disaster by interjecting a comment which causes the direction to shift. Similarly, this person keeps the discussion moving when there is a "stall" among the meeting participants. This person is an "observer," and it is this keen sense of observation which makes him or her so valuable.

4. **The Strategist.** This is the thinker with a "black-belt" in human relations. He or she handles people, identifies the motivations of individuals, and develops the approach and structures for the meetings, sales calls and presentations.

5. **The Intellectual Muscle.** These are often the "brainiacs" who are heavy-duty experts, but who may lack people skills. It is imperative that every team have subject-matter-experts who can match up with a prospect's counterparts on issues such as system design, engineering, and operations.

6. **The Closer.** The person with the authority to close the deal; work out the price, terms and related issues; and make the commitment on the part of the company. Big deals cannot be sold by a sales professional alone. It takes a tribe to hunt a big sale, and the chief of the tribe needs to lead the hunt.

While it's likely to have people capable of playing more than one role on your team, it is highly *unlikely* that the team will have "the complete package" in any one person.

But this situation is not unique to your own company – it's true of your competitors as well. Rather than focusing on trying to find the one person capable of filling all of the roles necessary in a complex sale to a major account, it's best to focus on those variables over which we can exert some control:

- **Ability to play as a part of a team.** Team members should be just that -- members of a team. They should play well with others when in the sandbox.

- **Familiarity with Sales Size and Duration of Sales Cycle.** Find those people who are accustomed to the length of the sales cycle and the size of the deals you're likely to secure. There really is a "rhythm" associated with the size of the sale and the duration of the sales cycle. There is a cadence. A measure. For example, every sales cycle has a peak. Indeed, some have multiple peaks. It can be disastrous if the customer is "peaking" and you or your team is out of synch.

- **"German shepherd" discipline.** When you are a part of a multi-person team, you need to be able to respond to the subtle leadership signals of "come," "go," "no," "sit" and "stay." Team members must know how to listen, particularly to queues unique to your company, your organization or your team.

And, as important as each of these roles may be, there is a far more important reason that a *team* is necessary to win large opportunities from major accounts. From our observation of, and participation in, literally hundreds of large "deals" with major accounts, one characteristic is almost universally consistent: While there are any number of people on the customer's "team" who have the authority to say "NO" – that is, they have "veto power," there is typically only one person on the customer team who can say "YES." Identifying this individual and ensuring that he or she is being sold to – while at the same time delicately balancing the requirement to meet the needs of those other team members with veto power – can generally only be accomplished through the efforts of a team working in harmony with a shared, or common, objective.

And while it is virtually always the case that only one person the team representing the customer or prospective customer who can say "YES," it is also virtually always the case that this executive will not act in isolation or independently of the other members on his or her team.

While the author is tempted at this point to articulate the broad negative consequences associated with such "consensus decision-making," or "lowest common denominator decision-making," it is far more productive to accept that this is a "given" in almost every significant sales opportunity with a major account and to determine how best to deal with this "given" in a manner which provides the highest likelihood of a "win."

Accepting such a premise quite naturally leads to a choice, which may be made implicitly or explicitly, but will be made: Should the team focus its efforts on the one person identified as being capable of saying "YES," or should the team focus its efforts on "winning over" as many members of the evaluation team which are likely to say "NO" as possible?

Our view is that the latter is the most responsible and prudent behavior to undertake. While admittedly not as "satisfying," clearing the table of as many likely "NO" votes as possible, is most likely to result in a decision in our favor. In our experience, it is the young, less-experienced, exuberant sales professional whose agenda is to "make a name for himself," that will result in a focus on the individual representing the customer which the sales team all agree is the one person who can say "YES."

The sales professional who adopts this approach is placing a bet. The bet is that the team member representing the customer, who all on the selling company's team agree is likely to be the one person who can say "YES," has an objective in common with our team's member who wants to "make a name for himself." What else would compel this person to make a decision in our favor when doing so would be contrary to the majority of his or her team members?

While being an observer of such theatrics may provide wonderful entertainment, such behavior is, at best, risky and, at worst, violating the individual's fiduciary responsibilities to his employer.

Gaining an Unfair Advantage
Chapter 2

Sales is inherently a profession that has a degree of "randomness" associated with it. Our objective is, to the degree possible, mitigate as much of the *random* nature of selling with a *purposeful* nature. The principles described in this book are all designed with this objective in mind.

Given this, it is acknowledged that there are times when a sales professional may close a deal, sign a new account or get a large order without much – or sometimes any – effort. Often referred to as "Blue Birds," there is no shame in this type of success and it should be celebrated and relished – but acknowledged for what it is.

Conversely, many times a sales professional will not close that deal, sign that new account or get that large order despite having put forth a great deal of effort and – arguably – is *deserving* of the win. Such is the nature of the profession.

There are times when someone else

within the sales professional's firm will attempt to denigrate or minimize these "Blue Birds." In fact, it may be that efforts are made not to pay the incentive compensation associated with these sales. Most often, these critics do not have a background in sales. When the critic or critics are also in sales, the feeling is often rooted in envy or sheer competitiveness. But over the course of a sales professional's career, these "Blue Birds" are generally offset by opportunities that the sales professional *did* deserve to win, but which were lost due to factors beyond his or her control.

"All other things being equal," there are as many reasons that a given sale is awarded to one sales professional over another as there are shades of gray. A sale can be won or lost based on anything ranging from the decision-maker being the brother-in-law of the decision-maker to the decision-maker feeling that he or she "owed" the sales professional an order because of the tickets he or she was given to the Super Bowl.

It's often said that "...people buy from people they like." And some sales professionals are more adept than others at developing a relationship with the buyer. Frequently, these relationships cross the line from "professional" to "personal." Frankly, we see nothing wrong with that, provided that no ethical breach is involved.

Again, "all other factors being equal," who wouldn't buy from the sales professional most liked or who has made the effort to develop a personal relationship?

Purposeful Selling™ is not an alternative to developing a personal or professional relationship with the decision-maker, influencer, gatekeeper or anyone else involved in the purchasing decision. Indeed, to the degree that the sales professional can establish such a relationship, he or she enhances the chances of winning a deal, getting an order or closing a new account. Using the principles of *Purposeful Selling*™ <u>and</u> having a personal or professional relationship with those involved in the buying decision provides the sales professional with an obvious advantage over his or her competitors.

The objective of the sales professional or sales team, however, is to eliminate the phrase "...all other things being equal..." from the buyer's decision. Using the principles of *Purposeful Selling*™ will put the seller in the position of having an *un-equal* advantage.

Chapter 3

"It's a numbers game. The more calls you make, the more appointments you'll get. The more appointments you get, the more sales you'll make. The more sales you make, the higher your income will be. It's simple, really. It's a numbers game."

There is a class of sales professional which spends most of his or her time on the phone. These particular sales professionals are variously known as Inside Sales, Tele-Sales, and Tele-Marketing or by a host of other "labels."

It's a tough job, and one that not everyone is cut out for.

I was first introduced to this concept in 1987, as I was about to leave IBM. A former IBM manager had accepted a position with a company which sold used or refurbished IBM mini-computers.

In 1987, IBM had not yet embraced this form of selling, and the concept was as foreign to me as if I'd been given a sales territory in Luxembourg – but I didn't speak the language.

At the time, I was a sales manager for one of IBM's largest customers, and our team had a quota of almost $140 million. In a good year, as the leader of a team responsible for one of IBM's flagship customers, my earnings were just shy of $90,000.

When my former manager called and suggested that I meet with her to discuss joining her new employer – thinking I had nothing to lose – I accepted the invitation.

After arriving, I spent some time with her top sales professional. Dressed in jeans and a tee-shirt and crammed into a space far too small for the size of the group, it was as close to what I imagined a "boiler-room" sales operation looking like.

A nice enough fellow, I could tell he was eager to get back on the phone and to stop "wasting his time" answering my banal questions. Before I let him get back to his phone, though, I had two questions that I <u>had</u> to get answered. One, how much did you make last year? "Two and a quarter. But it was an off year." Not wanting to make my ignorance too obvious, I left it at that without clarifying if he meant $225,000. $225,000. That was well over twice what I made – and I had a position of some considerable responsibility...or so I thought. The next question: Do you really sell exclusively over the phone? You never make a face-to-face sales call? Doesn't that bother you? "Sounds like it bothers **you**. I'd prefer to come to work dressed like this and not have to put on a suit. And besides, whatever time I spend out of the office translates into sales I'm *not* making. So no, it doesn't bother me one bit. Can I go now?"

It was a notion that, frankly, was just difficult for me to "wrap my head around." But quite obviously it was working for him and for his company. But simply because it was something that we didn't do at IBM (at least not then), it didn't *feel* right. Of course, IBM's tardiness in embracing this selling model is ultimately what caused it to get out of the typewriter and copier business. It simply wasn't cost-effective to send a $100,000 a year sales rep to make a sales call to sell one or two "IBM Correcting Selectric" typewriters. So, after IBM had hemorrhaged enough money, it sold that part of its business to a company which became known as Lexmark. Lexmark, not shackled by IBM's aversion to anything but "the IBM way," used a vastly different distribution model and turned the business into one which was finally profitable again.

Around the same time, I'd heard of a software company based in Houston, BMC, which hired a roomful of IBM sales folks, gave them a phone and a phonebook and told them to go sell some software. And while it may have been hard for these IBMers to adjust to selling exclusively over the phone, the "sting" was made less painful by the paychecks of $400-500,000/year that they were getting.

Now, of course, almost any company which uses a business model predicated on a low cost of selling embraces the phone-based model.

Now, of course, almost any company which uses a business model predicated on a low cost of selling embraces the phone-based model.

In fact, even those in "outside sales" still need to be adept at using the telephone in order to get an appointment or to "qualify" a lead.

Statistically, the average number of attempted telephone calls for every opportunity which eventually results in a sale is six. That means six times getting the "brush-off," getting no answer, being transferred to VoiceMail or leaving messages with a secretary which are never returned. Six. And that's for opportunities which eventually <u>do</u> result in a sale.

Given this, how *on earth* are we ever going to schedule our "research calls" or develop a "coach," much less schedule an appointment with the executive who is the ultimate decision-maker but who has never even <u>heard</u> of our company?

In today's reality, to be successful, a sales professional must answer these questions and overcome this challenge. And this is not even someone who makes his or her living selling over the phone – all he or she wants to do is get an appointment!

The keys? The first is by making yourself relevant to the person you're calling. Somehow you've got to cut through the clutter represented by all of the other vendors attempting to do the same thing that you are. And this is one of those times for which it may be appropriate to "wear your customer's shoes." In the "crazy-busy" chaotic world in which most executives operate, studies show that the amount of time you've got for catching the executive's attention is less than eight seconds. Eight seconds. 8. Take nine seconds and you've lost the executive's interest. So the second key: brevity. But being brief without making yourself relevant is a non-starter. So you've got to do both.

Let's look first at what won't work, but is done day-in and day-out by people who sell (or attempt to sell) over the phone:

"Is this Mr. Jones? Hi, this is Jane Gray with Manic Maids."

"We're offering a deal right now on commercial cleanings. Have you ever worked with a cleaning company before?"

How bad could Jane be? How much damage could Jane do after uttering only 30 words to Mr. Jones?

For starters, when your opening statement is something along the lines of "We're offering a deal right now!" you're putting the cart before the horse. There was no "problem" established to begin with, no context given. Your pitch comes off as exactly what it is: a generic script that shows no interest in the person on the receiving end (other than prying open his wallet). Why would anyone put in that position care if you have a deal right now – or ever?

Second, you have no idea if the person you are speaking to is qualified to make the decision on whether or not what you're offering is of value to them. So when the person says "No thanks, not interested" or "We're all set," you just got blown off by someone that quite possibly didn't have the authority to say "yes" in the first place.

Third, even if you are speaking to the decision maker, you immediately followed your opening statement with a probing question. This raises defenses and leads to terse one-word answers. You can just imagine feeling and hearing the prospect's resistance and tension over the phone. Think how you'd feel in the same situation: cornered, perhaps insulted and certainly interested only in hanging up the phone – noisily.

Maybe this "selling over the phone" stuff is a little more difficult than we assumed at first blush. How about one that's got a higher probability of success (but only slightly higher):

Hello, this is [NAME] from [COMPANY]. I'm hoping to talk to the head of the logistics department. (response) Great! Oh, before you transfer me, could you please give me the name and extension in case we get disconnected. Thank you so much for your help.1a. (If you get resistance here) Let me tell you just a bit about our technology and perhaps you could recommend what department I *should* be talking to. We have a product tracking technology so much more efficient than the RFID technology that you use now, it would save each of your stores over $1.25 million. I was assuming that this would be the logistics department, but perhaps you could steer me elsewhere?

(Now transferred to the correct person) Hi Mr. Prospect my name is [NAME] from [COMPANY], I was hoping to set up a time to talk with you about our new product tracking technology that can be used to dry and wet goods from underwear to crinkled up bags of frozen chicken nuggets. Initial tests show it as 28% more efficient and by our calculations, it should save each of your stores about $1.25 million per year. (pause as long as needed here until Mr. Prospect talks)2a. (If you get resistance here) Look, I understand that you are extremely busy. I also understand the awesome responsibility that you have in tracking each and every product in each and every store on the globe and on every truck and in every warehouse. If you give me a ten-minute meeting and we can't convince each other that there's a possible match here, I'll do the honor of throwing myself out the door. (again, long pause here)

Fantastic, I'm going to be somewhat in your area in two weeks, would you have 10-minutes the morning of the 22nd?

Again, how much damage can be done? Oh, where to even begin?!

Let's try a third (and final) approach:

Hi, is this Phil Jones? Hi Phil, my name is Joe Salesguy with NameYourCompany. Our firm works with industrial ceramics providers similar to your company. We've learned that many of these customers are having difficulty – even with ceramic media, of grinding dense metals to achieve particles below 5 microns. Does your firm have a similar problem? (YES) We've developed a new patented technology which achieves these levels of granularity, and our customers which are using it are reporting that their energy costs are being reduced by 31% and that their product consistency has been improved by 26% on average. If these kinds of results sound interesting to you, I'd like to suggest that we set up an appointment for about 45 minutes which will allow me to describe how this new technology may work in your environment. I'm going to be in your area next Thursday afternoon. I have availability at 2:00 or 3:30 that afternoon. Which would be better for you?

What did our sales professional do differently this time? He quickly established his relevance (we have experience working with companies like yours) and piqued the interest of the person called by citing "real world" results.

In reality, there is a subset of those called who will begin saying "I'm not interested..." before they've even heard your name. You could be giving away $100 bills, and they wouldn't be interested. But most rational people, upon hearing results such as those cited, would gladly spare 45 minutes to learn more. Relevance. Brevity.

There are many different schools of thought about telephone selling. One was described at the outset of this chapter: it's a numbers game. The other primary school of thought is that by investing some time in advance of the call to conduct a small amount of research will aid the caller in being more relevant. And frankly, given the ease with which this research can be conducted – believe it or not, there was a time before "Google" – not doing at least a minimal amount of research in advance of a call is, if not shameful, unprofessional. Social networks, particularly LinkedIn, also are a veritable "treasure trove" of information to assist in establishing relevance. LinkedIn, in particular, has two unique benefits: 1) It shows if you know someone who knows the person you're calling – this can be helpful, for example, in requesting that someone make an introduction; and 2) It shows the person's career and education background as well as personal interests. This information can be valuable fodder as "conversation starters."

Since using the phone is a "given," even for those who don't "sell" directly over the phone, the prudent sales professional will make the effort to improve his or her telephone skills so that he or she can maintain that "edge" – however nominal or incremental – which provides valuable separation from the rest of the "pack."

Case Study 1
<u>Chapter 4</u>

"And, based on your agreement with what we've just discussed, I would propose that you assign a team responsible for implementing our system. Based on the ROI that we reviewed, the longer we wait, the less impact we will have."

The sales professional stood confidently next to the presentation easel as the president of the division sat pensively for what seemed like an eternity. The president had invited his entire executive team to the presentation and proposal. Was he embarrassed that he'd wasted their time? Was he unsure of whether to agree? Did he feel as though he was being asked to make a hasty decision? All of these thoughts went fleeting through the sales professional's mind.

Finally, the president turned around and faced his executive team which was seated around the mahogany conference room table. "I wish all of you understood our business as well as the young man standing in front of us today.

Tom, I'm appointing you as head of a task force to get this system implemented within ninety days. You have access to anyone in the company you need." And then he wheeled his chair around and faced the sales professional, still standing confidently next to the flip chart stand he'd used for the presentation. "Well done. Is there anything else?"

The sales executive said, "No sir. I look forward to working with Tom and the team he puts together. Thanks for your support and confidence in our firm and our solution." As the president stood up to leave the meeting, he faced the sales executive, locked eyes with him, and said "I'm not doing this because of my confidence in your company or your solutions, but because of my confidence in you. Don't let me down!"

How did our sales professional get to this point? How did he get a meeting with the division president? Moreover, how did he get an order for over $2 million without "asking for the order?" Did he just call the president's office and tell him he wanted to meet with him?

Hardly. The meeting was the culmination of weeks of hard work and conscientious effort by the sales professional. He used three fundamental principles which will be discussed in this book and which are part of what we refer to as *Purposeful Selling*™.

When I began my career in sales, I had the good fortune of working for IBM and Hewlett-Packard, two "household name" firms with stellar reputations. And so, when I called Bill Starkey, the President of GTE, and asked his secretary for an appointment, I was not surprised when she provided me with two or three times that Mr. Starkey would be available to meet. I took this for granted. Why *wouldn't* Bill Starkey meet with me?

It was in an interview with Jim Thanos, the Vice President of Sales for a small start-up, Metaphor, and one of the best sales executives on the planet, who explained his views to me an our first meeting. "George, what you need to understand is this: When you work for IBM or H-P, the customer is "buying the company" first, "buying the product" second, and "buying you" last. But if you come to work for a small company like Metaphor, a company that your prospect has probably never heard of, the customer is "buying the company" – Metaphor – last. Secondly, he's "buying the product." And the first thing he's buying? He's "buying you."

It was many years later that I connected Jim's sage advice with the ease of my getting an appointment with Bill Starkey at GTE. But over the years, Jim's advice has proven to be true many times over. And unfortunately, the "truth" in his advice manifests itself like a pot of ice-cold water being thrown in my face – every single time I fail to get a desired appointment!

But why *wouldn't* the president of a multi-billion dollar company meet with me? I'd never met Bill Starkey before I requested a meeting, and he didn't hesitate.

In fact, as I reflected upon my experience as either a sales professional or as a sales manager at IBM and Hewlett-Packard, I could not recall a single instance when an executive from a prospective customer had *ever* refused my request for a meeting.

"Mr. Devitt, welcome to selling as the *rest of the world* knows it." The days were over when all I had to do was pick up the phone to get an appointment with anyone I chose in any company I chose. Disheartening? You bet. Did I take it personally? Absolutely. Had I done a single thing to *earn the right* to a meeting? Nope.

But how had the sales professional who I'd just observed making a presentation – after which the division president not only said "YES," but told his direct-reports "that he wished all of them understood their business as well as the young man who just completed the presentation – how had he gotten a meeting in the President's private conference room? <u>His</u> employer was hardly a "household name."

He had followed the principles outlined in this book, thoroughly knew his customer upside and down and had the ability to communicate <u>precisely</u> how his company could help the customer deal with its "pain points."

Case Study 2

Chapter 5

Hewlett-Packard has always been one of "America's Most Admired Companies" due to the respect and dignity afforded its employees and the firm's leadership in technical innovation.

Unfortunately, despite the company's overwhelming domination in the market for "technical computing," the firm had never achieved similar levels of success in the commercial, or business, market for computers.

And it was into this environment that I joined the firm early in 1988. One executive, Ray Drost, was committed to making an earnest effort to change this situation. Ray agreed to fund a small team as part of a "Skunkworks" project, with the objective of penetrating the commercial market in the Western U.S.

There were four of us which made up the team, and based on some market analysis, we determined that our target market would be the financial services industry – specifically, banking. As circumstances would have it, there were four dominant banks in California at that time: Bank of America, Wells Fargo, Security Pacific and First Interstate. A team of four and four large banks. Already our decision about where to focus our efforts was looking prescient.

I happened to draw the straw which said "First Interstate Bank." Prior to this project, my knowledge of banking and the banking industry was limited to who had the least expensive checking accounts.

While First Interstate had not purchased a single computer from Hewlett-Packard (ever!), it was assumed that the bank had thousands of H-P's market-dominating LaserJet printers and its advanced hand-held calculators. But since these products were sold through channel partners and not by H-P directly, the number and location of these products was totally unknown – and, as one former Secretary of Defense would say – "unknowable."

And, as hard as it may be for some readers to believe, this was before something known as the World Wide Web even existed. A recent transplant to California from Florida, I didn't even have a network of acquaintances whom I could draw on to ask for an introduction. After perusing the bank's Annual Report and other SEC filings, as well as requesting a D&B report on the bank, I was at a standstill with absolutely no idea of how I was to "penetrate" this behemoth of a bank.

Lacking any better ideas and since I had not already transferred my checking account from Florida to California, I walked into the Marina del Rey First Interstate branch office and opened an account. Given the dearth of my knowledge of the bank, I had an unquenchable thirst for information of <u>any</u> type.

After opening my account, I asked to meet the branch manager. I estimated that she was about 25 years old and her bearing gave me the impression that this was probably her first job after graduating from college. She was kind enough to invite me into her office and to sit down. Little did she know that she was about to be "peppered" with questions until a) she kicked me out, or b) the branch closed, or c) I ran out of questions. Option (c) was not likely.

While I should have been better prepared, with a list of questions written out in advance, I was so ignorant that questions were not in short supply. I began by asking her who I called if I had a question or needed to do something – such as re-order checks. Quite proudly, she explained that I did not call the branch, but that First Interstate had led the market by establishing "Tele-Service Centers" which could be called 24 hours a day, 7 days a week. I asked how many such centers there were and where the nearest was located. She explained that the bank had established six such centers located throughout the state and that the nearest Center in proximity to Marina del Rey was in City of Industry, California.

I brazenly asked if she would allow me to impose upon her to arrange for me to visit and tour the Center in City of Industry. She answered my request with a question: "Have you ever been to City of Industry?" I answered that I was new to Los Angeles and had not, but was curious as to why she asked. She replied simply that the Center was not located in one of Los Angeles' more desirable areas. In other words, City of Industry was the "armpit" of Los

Angeles. Nonetheless, she was polite enough to call the manager of the Center who happily agreed to give me a tour of the Center. My *Purposeful Selling*™ "research calls" were about to commence!

Finding my way to the Center (the reader will be reminded that not only had the World Wide Web yet come into existence, GPS devices were as rare as "web sites"), I was greeted cordially. And, indeed, the bank had made every effort to minimize its investment in real estate by locating the Center in an area not suitable for habitation. The Center itself, however, was a state-of-the-art facility. Quite literally without anything better to do, I made it my goal to be the Center Manager's new "best friend." What he probably assumed would be a brief tour ultimately developed to be my primary workplace.

I learned that there were six such Centers around the state (interstate banking had not yet been legalized), and that the number of in-bound calls had grown rapidly and, in the prior month, surpassed the "one million" milestone for the number of collective calls to all of the Centers.

I observed each "agent" as they went about their business: making address changes, processing "stop payment" orders for checks, re-ordering checks, responding to balance inquiries and a variety of other simple tasks that had previously been performed at the branches by people either calling the branch or visiting it in person. Not only were the Centers saving the bank money, but they were also improving the level of service provided to its customers.

Eventually, I became a "fixture" in the City of Industry Center. I knew almost every agent by name and had endeared myself to them by bringing two dozen doughnuts to the Center every morning.

After about two months, I developed enough "nerve" to ask if I could sit in one of the agent's "stations" and take some in-bound calls.

While initially reluctant – bankers are not known as being big risk-takers – he came to the conclusion that I could be rather persistent and that it was in <u>his</u> best interests to allow me to take some calls. Because I had observed the agents for so long, I didn't even require training.

While my establishing a "camp site" within the bank caused me to draw undeserved praise and recognition, I was approaching the point where I knew I would need to <u>do</u> something or I would wear out my welcome.

There is an old banking adage that the duration of a customer's relationship with the bank correlates in an exponential fashion to the number of "products" provided by the bank to the customer. For example, if someone has only a checking account, the average duration of the relationship with that customer is one year. If the customer has a checking account and a savings account, the customer is likely to stay with the bank for four years. And if the customer has a checking account, a savings account and a credit card issued by the bank, that customer will – on average – stay with the bank for nine years. Thus, the environment for "cross-selling" was fertile and demonstrably beneficial.

As rare as web sites on the World Wide Web and GPS devices was the number of installations of Customer Relationship Management systems

(CRM). This is not particularly surprising, as CRM software, as a category, did not yet exist.

But despite the fact that the project which I envisioned hadn't yet been developed or even given a name, I began its germination.

In an action with some degree of boldness associated with it, I requested a meeting with Ray Drost – the executive sponsor of what we came to call the "Commercial Account Pilot Program." It was in this meeting that I gave a "mock" presentation of my concept. Without props or even a formal presentation, but in as animated a fashion as I was capable, I began my "somewhat extemporaneous" presentation by explaining the correlation between the duration of a customer's relationship with the number of accounts the customer has with that bank.

I followed this with a discussion regarding the lack of marketing prowess among banks, which is widely acknowledged within the marketing community. I then gave examples of typical bank marketing practices, which are largely limited to the use of "statement stuffers," tele-marketing in the evening hours and providing "teaser rates" for credit cards or a variety of loan products – none of which is associated with any success of note.

Then, in my most earnest attempt at creating "high drama," I said (while this is from memory and is not a precise rendition of my statements, the point is conveyed adequately):

"And, despite the vast sums spent on what are essentially "fruitless" marketing campaigns, The Bank is missing over one million QUALIFIED sales opportunities each and every month."

At this point I took a seat next to a computer monitor – with the monitor facing me and not visible to Ray or the others watching the presentation.

"Yes, Mrs. Smith, I can help you with that. First, let's begin with your account number. Do you have that handy? (Pause) Excellent. Do you know the check number that you wish to have the "stop payment" order applied to? (Pause) Great. And do you remember the amount of the check? (PAUSE) Excellent. Well, Mrs. Smith, I've taken care of your "stop payment" request and that should take effect within one hour. Is there anything else I can help you with? No?

Before I let you go, Mrs. Smith, while we were waiting on that doggone slow computer, I happened to notice that you've had an average daily balance of $7,211 sitting in a non-interest-bearing checking account for the last three months? Might I suggest that you move $2,000 of that into a Certificate of Deposit on which you will earn 7% interest? (PAUSE) Yes, ma'am. I think that makes a lot of sense. And of course, those funds which you move into the CD will have the same FDIC insurance as your other funds.   Can I process that now for you? Wonderful, let me just do a few more things – this'll just take a minute. Great. I'm all done and those funds have been moved. You'll be receiving a form in the mail which you just need to sign and send back.   We even provide an envelope with a stamp already on it! Well, you're very welcome, Mrs. Smith.   We value your business with First Interstate Bank."

Standing up, I explain that "in the background," our computer is reaching out into the array of "spaghetti systems" that we have: one for mortgage loans, a different one for credit cards, another one for checking – which of course is different than the one we use for savings, and consolidating the records associated with all of the relationships Mrs. Smith has with First Interstate. Then, through our "Artificial Intelligence System," it makes a recommendation for the agent to offer the customer. Now, Ray, there's some very powerful psychology at work here. First, Mrs. Smith called us...we didn't call her. Second, I was just in the role of 'problem solver' when I assisted her with the 'stop-payment' request. Third, before hanging up I make an 'oh, by the way' suggestion – now Mrs. Smith doesn't think I'm selling to her. She thinks I'm still just helping her. The whole dynamic of our interaction is shifted – I'm just continuing to help Mrs. Smith, so that almost-reflexive, very natural 'wall' that goes up for most of us when she answers the phone and finds out she's being sold to – that 'wall' never goes up. And last month the bank had over one million of its customers call us for 'help.' And that's one million lost sales opportunities which are warm leads – heck, they're better than warm leads – one million opportunities which are lost forever."

As I take my seat again, I tell Ray that the reason for requesting our meeting is because I am asking him to invest $50,000 in a pilot program at The Bank, which they customer will match, dollar-for-dollar, to develop the system that you just "saw" me demonstrate. I've asked for the order, and as they teach in Sales School 101, I'm now silently awaiting Ray's response.

"Who would you present this to?" he asked.

"The Bank's Chief Marketing Officer is a woman named Mary Bankston. I've not met her, but I have developed a relationship with a consultant who is on a retainer and assigned full-time to her personally. I've already discussed this notion – in very broad terms – with this consultant, who I'm confident would open the door for a meeting with Ms. Bankston."

"All right, Devitt. You've got your 50-grand. Now go get a whopper of an order and don't make me look bad."

Now, to fast-forward, I took all of my "research" notes and developed a formal presentation which followed the *Purposeful Selling*™ model. On the "Next Steps" portion of the presentation, I asked for her to match H-P's $50,000 investment and to approve the development of a pilot. She agreed, but said, "I may need for you to make one more presentation before we get the final signoff…hang on just a minute." She stepped out of her office and returned in 2-3 minutes. "What are you doing this Thursday at 1:30 in the afternoon?" I responded with "What do I <u>need</u> to be doing at 1:30 on Thursday?" She said she wanted me to give the exact same presentation on Thursday, but she didn't tell me who the audience would be. After we adjourned our meeting – and with everyone, from the Bank and from H-P, almost giddy – I asked Ms. Bankston's consultant who I'd be presenting to. "Bill Siart," she said. Siart was the Chairman, President and CEO of First Interstate Bancorp.

The pilot was an overwhelming success and ultimately the Bank invested over $20 million in H-P products and services to implement the first CRM system ever in a financial services institution. Of course, we weren't clever enough to call it that – but that's exactly what it was.

In the end, I left Hewlett-Packard to go to work at a small start-up software firm, and never reaped one dime in commissions. I was gone for over a year before the system went "live," and First Interstate became one of H-P's "Showcase Accounts." Ray Drost's instincts about the company's viability in the commercial market were proven to be correct. Mary Bankston was promoted to Chief Operating Officer of the Bank, which was ultimately acquired by Wells Fargo Bank. Because she was able to monetize her stock options upon the bank's acquisition, she retired at age 40.

"Nuanced" Questioning
Chapter 6

But let's not start at the end – let's go back to the beginning. Selling a high-ticket and complex solution isn't about deciding whether the sales professional should use the "Puppy Dog Close" or the "Rolling Pen Close." Selling in a complex environment requires a unique set of skills and the discipline to follow a set of guiding principles.

The first of the principles that are part of the *Purposeful Selling*™ program is the very fundamental premise that **our customers buy from us not because of how much they know about our products or services, but because of how much we know about their business and our ability to solve their problems**. Seems simple enough. And in sales training workshops, I always get a lot of head nodding when I present this principle. "Tell me something I don't know," said one seasoned sales professional, arms crossed in front of himself.

But despite the fact that most experienced sales professionals know this, they don't "walk the talk." Observe them or observe yourself when you're with customers. Your time with customers is, by and large, spent talking about a new product or a new feature or a price reduction.

It's almost always about *your* company and its products. It's generally not spent learning the customer's business – and specifically what the business's "pain points" are.

More often than not, it's not spent asking probing questions about your customer's business challenges – or "pain points." And getting to this point isn't as easy as asking a friendly customer to lunch, "Hey, what are your pain points?" A confused look and a "Huh?" is likely what the questioner will get. Most individuals within our customers' organizations don't think in these terms on a day-to-day basis.

But to be successful in learning the customer's business, the sales professional has to master the skills necessary to gain this information. And a "frontal assault" isn't likely to be effective. The approach used has to be more nuanced. Why? Because when the average low-level or mid-level employee, when asked "What are your company's goals and objectives?" is likely to think the questioner has rocks in his head. It's a conversation which simply doesn't feel natural.

And yet, without knowing the answer to that question, there's no way the sales professional can present his or her products or solution in a way which solves the customer's problems.

So – What Defines a "Major Account?"

Chapter 7

As mentioned in the Foreword, this book is about the complex sale – and how to approach it.

It's not about selling skills, *per se*. There are plenty of other books, seminars or other means to learn "closing skills" and "elevator pitches" and other selling "techniques." This book is written for the sales professional or sales manager who wants to be in the position of "trusted advisor" to his or her customer. It's not written for someone who's looking for the next best "technique." While there is a place for learning "techniques," this isn't it.

Regardless of the industry, the practices and disciplines which are outlined here apply – provided that the sale is complex in nature. And characteristically, these sales typically have a long sales cycle. How is complexity defined? Quite simply, that there are many "moving parts" and dynamics at play in the sales process. And these may come from your own company or from the customer, or, most likely – from both.

This type of complexity is typified by having to get concurrence from many different people in a wide range of departments and levels within your customer's organization. Often, this complexity is because there are many people who can say "no" to a proposal, but there's generally only one person who can say "yes." Or the complexity may result because you're trying to put together a solution for your customer that incorporates product lines from several divisions of your own company. And these sales are typically measured in the millions of dollars and may result in contracts spanning five years or more. The sales cycle for this type of sale is typically measured in months or years. But it has been our experience that this process – if executed properly – will likely result in shortening the duration of the sales cycle.

In the example cited in the previous chapter, the customer was a multi-billion dollar petroleum company. The account had never done business with this sales professional's company before. And the path was littered with other sales professionals who'd tried. It was a "target account" – winning it would be a game-changer for the sales team and for its company. His predecessors had presented a vast array of the company's products to the prospect – *hoping* that at least one of them would stick. But as any good sales executive will attest, "hope is not a strategy." In fact, it's impossible to know what products to sell until we've mastered the first principle of *Purposeful Selling*™ – thoroughly understanding our customer's business and how we can solve the customer's problems – those "pain points" referred to earlier.

This may seem like stating the obvious. But when the customer interactions of most sales professionals are examined critically, most often their time with the customer is spent in a discussion of his company's newest product or price incentive or promotion. So while we acknowledge that it is stating the obvious, most sales professionals don't "walk the talk" in their daily interactions with customers. But they can "walk the talk" by mastering and using this first principle.

Throughout the *Purposeful Selling*™ sales cycle, we must keep in mind that our objective is to understand the goals, objectives, strategies and tactics of our client. And then to identify the challenges, impediments, obstacles and inhibitors that are standing in the way of our customer achieving its goals and objectives. It's only after we do this that we can logically map a solution from our product set which supports the attainment of the customer's goals and objectives. *So we start at the beginning with the end in mind.*

Research
Chapter 8

When a prospect was assigned to another sales professional, the first thing he did was research the company as thoroughly as possible – *before* making his first phone call. He scoured the web, trade publications, social networking web sites such as LinkedIn, Dun & Bradstreet...anything he could get his hands on to develop a familiarity of his customer. As he did this, he looked specifically for information about the company's strategic objectives, its direction, its imperatives, its organization. While this is essential, we should be cautious that we don't fall into "analysis paralysis." There comes a point that we need to finish this type of research and start meeting with the customer to do some "primary research."

But in this case, who would he call? Since his company had never done business with this customer, there wasn't a stack of business cards he could draw on or names in his company's CRM (Customer Relationship Management) system that had any history. In a quandary, he started asking around the office if anyone knew someone at his account. He asked his friends. He used LinkedIn to see if there were connections that could be made. He just needed a friendly introduction to *anyone* within his client's organization, whether their department was related to his products and services or not. He finally found a neighbor who'd worked for the company several years earlier and was happy to make an introduction to his former boss. So, he had his "in!" And he carefully scripted his first call, which would be a request for an in-person meeting.

"Hi Bill. I'm John Smith with Acme Corporation and we have a mutual friend, my neighbor Jack Tatum. Did Jack tell you that I'd be calling?" He had started the process. "Great. Well, to be perfectly candid, I've been assigned as the sales executive from my company responsible for your business, but we haven't done a lot of business together in the past. In fact, all I know about your company is what I could glean from your Annual Report, your web site and other third-party sources. It would mean a lot to me if you could spare an hour to meet with me and just give me an overview of your firm. When would be a convenient time for you to meet with me – and by the way: I promise I'm not going to try to sell you anything!"

When John met with Bill, he had two objectives in mind: learning how the company was organized and getting the names of other people he could meet with in this non-threatening, non-selling environment. In every meeting – research meetings, really – John would ask for other names of people he could meet with. After several meetings, John started asking questions which would allow him to identify the prospect's goals and objectives – and the inhibitors to achieving them.

It's important to note that customers don't always think this way – particularly if they're far down in the organizational structure. Despite this, these are excellent people to conduct research calls with. This brings us to the second fundamental principle of *Purposeful Selling*™: that **we sell top – down, but we thoroughly research the customer from the bottom – up.** Part of the mastery of this research is finding indirect ways of asking questions which will provide the information we're seeking. Remember, we're beginning with the end in mind.

In our early meetings – and we're careful not to refer to our meetings as "sales calls," but rather "research calls" – we're trying to learn some fundamental things about the customer: its organization, its competitors, its key initiatives, its culture. But eventually our meetings will delve further into the companies goals, objectives, strategies and tactics – and the challenges, obstacles, inhibitors or other "pain points" which may be standing in the way of achieving the customer's high level goals.

In these research calls, it's generally not going to be fruitful to ask "What are your organization's goals and objectives?" But using some creativity, we can get to the answer. For example, suppose the company's CEO is named Mr. Arthur. One question might be, "At the end of the year, if Mr. Arthur were to get a report card, what are the things he'd be graded on?" Similarly, it may be awkward to ask "What are your company's problems?"   But simply by rephrasing the question to "When Mr. Arthur was driving to the office this morning, what do you think were the three things he was most concerned about?"   Or, "If Mr. Arthur had trouble going to sleep last night, what do you think were the three things keeping him up?"

A fundamental rule during the research calls is that we resist the temptation to "sell" – even when the situation cries out for it! Another fundamental rule is that most of the time is spent with the customer talking – and we're asking open-ended and probing questions – and follow-up questions. In general, we adhere to the "90-10 Rule" – that is, the customer talks 90% of the time and we speak only 10% of the time, with the objective being that our 10% is spent asking questions. Realistically, though, we should anticipate our customer contact to be curious about why we're asking so many questions. We should also anticipate that the customer contact may be curious about what we do or what our products and services are. The sales professional should be prepared for this. Regarding the first question, often if we simply repeat the first principle of *Purposeful Selling*™ – that our company believes that customers buy from us not (so much) because of what they know about our products, but because of how much we know about their business and how our products may solve their problems. And it's natural for the customer to be curious about our business – so we should have a succinct, crisp and *brief* answer.

Throughout our series of research calls, we should be alert for people who are particularly helpful and sympathetic to our research project. These are people who we may call upon later as "coaches" or "internal advocates." They're the kind of people we'd be able to call later on the phone to get clarification on a particular point. They should also be familiar with the "politics" within our customer's organization. They may know who's really in a position of power – although this may not be reflected on a formal organization chart. They probably know who the "rising stars" are. They also may know who has the ear of the CEO. It doesn't hurt to develop a personal relationship with these individuals – outside of work, perhaps. For example, these are people you may invite to a ball game or golf outing.

During the research meetings, it's important to ask questions about your customer's competitors. From your customer's viewpoint, who are their competitors? What are their strengths? Their weaknesses? Is there one which is "up and coming" which may be a particular threat to your customer's business? We've worked with sales professionals who've conducted research on their customers' competitors to better understand their own customer.

Not all of the information that we gain in the research calls will relate to our products. But we should note examples of major business challenges that are far afield from our own business. It will give us credibility with the person we're meeting with because it will be obvious that our questions are not self-serving. And it's information we may use later.

The Executive Presentation
<u>Chapter 9</u>

This brings us to the third and final principle of *Purposeful Selling*™: that **a formal presentation to the decision-making executive is critical to establishing a long-term partnership and success with the customer.** All of the research that we've conducted – on our own (secondary research) or in our research calls (primary research) – culminates in this presentation. And it is in this presentation that we draw a logical path from the business our own company is in to our customer's challenges, obstacles, impediments, inhibitors and pain points. And if we're in the business of addressing these, we can logically draw a path which helps the customer see that by solving its challenges, we thereby help the customer to accomplish its strategies and achieve its goals and objectives. If done properly, there shouldn't even need to be a "close." It should be obvious that there are good reasons for our two companies to do business.

Clearly, a successful presentation to the executive is critical to our success. And orchestrating the executive presentation can often be a challenging task – even getting on his or her calendar is likely to be a difficult. Hopefully, during the course of our "research calls," we've developed a network of advocates, or "coaches." Ideally, we would call on our "coach" and ask him or her to set up the meeting for us.

In implementing the third principle, our preparation must be perfect. The presentation should be the culmination of all of the primary and secondary research we've conducted. It should flow logically. It should be well-rehearsed. Transitions should be seamless. It should always be reviewed with our "coach" or with multiple "coaches." They should be able to alert us to sensitive subjects or topics we should avoid. They can provide insight to ensure its accuracy.

The presentation itself is likely to cover the following areas. In fact, while it's obviously appropriate at times to stray from this agenda, it has served the author well many, many times.

Why? Because it speaks to "universal truths" that virtually <u>any</u> for-profit endeavor faces.

<u>Agenda</u>

Review of <Customer Name>'s Goals
and Objectives

Key Challenges Facing <Customer Name>

The Business of <Our Company Name>

Business-to-Business Alignment

Summary

Proposed Next Steps/Action Items

Let's "unpack" each of these topical areas. Before we begin, we thank the executive for his or her time and confirm how much time has been set aside for the meeting. We then review the agenda for the meeting. Note, that we don't even mention anything about our company until we're halfway through the presentation. People refer a lot to being "customer-focused." This presentation format gives meaning to those two words.

As we review each topic, it's imperative that we not give the impression that we know more about the executive's business than he or she does. While this seems plainly obvious, we've observed more than one sales professional come across as too "cocky" in the presentation, with a "let me tell you about your business..." tone. And while some may argue that there is a fine line between "confidence" and "cockiness," careful and repeated rehearsals should identify whether this will be an issue or not. We avoid this peril by carefully phrasing each topic on the agenda as we review it. For example, we may begin by saying "This is the agenda we'd propose for our meeting today. We'd like to begin by reviewing – based on our research – what your goals and objectives are. Then we'd like to discuss our understanding of some of the critical challenges facing your company. After that, we'd like to tell you a little bit about our company and follow that up with a discussion of how our business may align with yours and how we may be able to help you overcome some of the challenges you face, thus enabling you to accomplish your goals and objectives. And if we've done our job right and you concur, we'd like to suggest some potential next steps or action items." We'd then conclude with a question to gain concurrence, such as "Does this seem like a reasonable agenda for us to follow?"

At the end of each topical area, we attempt to ensure we're on track by asking something along the lines of "Does our understanding accurately capture your goals and objectives for <Company Name>? Have we missed anything? Is there anything you'd care to elaborate on?" Our objective is to get buy-in from the executive at every point along the way.

Clearly, the executive knows far more about his or her business than we do. And, as mentioned earlier, we will have rehearsed this presentation with our sales manager and with our "coach" several times before delivering it to the executive.

There are many schools of thought regarding the medium to use for the presentation. Most sales professionals will use PowerPoint and an LCD projector. But bear in mind that doing so will require that the lights be dimmed and the room be darkened. This will result in difficulty in making eye contact and reading the executive's body language. It also tends to make the viewer drowsy! If PowerPoint is used, it's imperative that the presenter deliver a high-energy, fast-paced presentation. We also recommend that the presenter stand next to the screen so he or she can make eye contact with the executive and any others who may be in attendance.

Although somewhat anachronistic, we've seen many effective presentations done with flip charts – particularly charts put together by a professional artist or graphic designer. Why might this be an effective medium? First, because it's uncommon. When the executive and anyone he or she invites to the meeting, the first thing they see upon entering the room is a flip chart stand with the cover chart depicting the company's logo - drawn by a professional artist. Secondly, the use of flip charts doesn't require that the lights be darkened – and avoids the disadvantages of doing so. Lastly, the presenter stands next to the flip chart stand. The audience's eyes can't avoid seeing the presenter – and their eyes and body language can't avoid being seen *by* the presenter! It also makes it easy to modify the charts based on feedback from the executive or other members of the audience.

The last chart in the presentation – after the executive has agreed that there is a potentially good business fit between the two companies – is the one containing Action Items and Next Steps. It doesn't hurt to be assumptive and to already have some action items on the slide or chart, using the format of Action Item, Responsible Party and Date as column headings. The first Action Item will likely be "Determine if a business fit exists between <Customer Name> and <Your Company Name>" with the date of the presentation and the sales professional's name already filled in. After that, the next item added to the Action Items/Next Steps will be dependent upon the success (or lack of success) of the presentation. If it went well, it may be appropriate to ask the executive to name a project manager to scope the implementation of what's being proposed. Similarly, since the Sales Manager is likely to be in attendance, he or she should also assign a project manager to work with the one assigned by the customer.

Sometimes it's a good idea to ask the executive when he or she would like to see the project implemented. After all, if you've presented a compelling business case, he or she will want it completed sooner rather than later. If you start with this date and work backwards in documenting the logical steps and deadlines for the high level tasks necessary to meet the deadline, one of the tasks is going to be to place an order for your products or services. So an "assumptive close" is part of the Action Items – and the sales professional never has to "ask for the order." Lastly, it's always a good idea to suggest regular progress checkpoints with the executive – even if they're quarterly – "to keep him (or her) abreast of the project and its progress." This leaves the door open for future meetings with this key executive so that a relationship can be developed over time.

Case Study 3
Chapter 10

A seasoned sales professional was assigned a multi-national account – an internationally recognized carbonated beverage company. The customer was already an established user of the selling company's products and services. Indeed, it was a multi-million dollar account.

While adoption of the selling company's products and services was strong in North America (where the customer's headquarters is), certain international markets were slow to implement the company's solutions, even though they were "standards" as defined by the headquarters offices. One particularly large market which had not adhered to the "standards" was a part of the customer's European operations, specifically the Spain/Portugal Region.

The sales professional's "coach" at the headquarters location believed that the Regional General Manager was not opposed to implementing the recommended solution, but that lower-level staffers were putting up obstacles and had not made it a priority. Based on this, the Account Manager asked his "coach" if he could arrange for a conference call with the Regional General Manager and the two of them. On the conference call, it was suggested that the Account Manager would travel to Madrid for a week to meet with the staff at the Regional Headquarters, and then end the week with a formal presentation to the Regional GM outlining a business case to implement his company's solution. The Regional GM readily agreed, after which the Account Manager's "coach" requested that the GM have his Executive Assistant set up meetings in advance with the key staffers involved.

The Account Manager flew to Madrid on the Sunday before Labor Day – knowing that this Monday would not be a holiday for the customer's employees in Spain. On Monday morning, he made his way to the customer's Regional Headquarters for a brief introductory meeting with the Regional GM. He then met with the GM's Executive Assistant and was given the schedule of meetings. They would begin on Monday afternoon and end late on Wednesday.

In his mind, he thought that this would work out well. He could use Wednesday night to review and consolidate his meeting notes and prepare a rough draft of the presentation. Hoping he would identify at least one "coach" in the process of the many meetings, he thought Thursday would be a good day to review the presentation with his "coach" and to rehearse. The presentation was already on the General Manager's calendar for 9:00AM Friday morning.

The Account Manager, already well-versed in his client's organization on a general level, set out to learn the organization of the Spain/Portugal Region. After he had developed a good understanding of the Region's organization and dynamics – and who the shining stars were and who had the ear of the General Manager – he was ready to start asking more probing questions related to the business.

Beginning with the end in mind – the end being the Executive Presentation to the General

Manager on Friday – the Account Manager began using the questioning skills he had developed by using the *Purposeful Selling*™ process with other parts of the customer's organization. His objective was to determine the Region's goals, objectives, strategies, tactics – and the challenges, obstacles, impediments, problems and inhibitors that stood in the way of achieving those goals and objectives.

When the staffers he conducted his research calls on learned that he wasn't "selling," but trying to learn the Region's business so that he could better support them, most opened up. In fact, one department manager was particularly helpful and suggested key people that the Account Manager should meet with that were not on his schedule. He invited that manager and his wife to dinner and developed him as a "coach" – someone he could trust and use to clarify and validate what he'd learned from his meetings.

He learned that conducting business in Spain is very different than it is in the United State. He was fortunate that everyone with whom he met spoke English – probably because the company was based in the United States. But "normal" business hours in Spain were quite different! The Account Manager noticed that hardly anyone got into the office before 9:30AM. And lunch breaks were later than he was used to. And longer. And while he didn't see anyone sleeping at work, there was the traditional mid-afternoon "siesta" that almost everyone took. But most people worked late, as well. It took some adjustment. As did eating dinner in restaurants in Madrid. Most of them didn't even **open** until 9:00PM!

On Wednesday evening, the Account Manager began to assemble and organize all of his notes from the research meetings he'd conducted. The GM had graciously allowed him to use a large conference room as his "work area" during the week. The conference table was literally covered with stacks of neatly ordered meeting notes. He began by starting with a blank sheet of paper and putting "Agenda" at the top of the page – and nothing else.

The next sheet of paper he entitled "Goals and Objectives." The answers he got from the people he met with ranged from quantifiable revenue and profit goals for the Region to more subjective goals such as "Ensuring a High Level of Bottler Satisfaction." He wrote down all of them, knowing he'd probably have to "whittle down" the list.

On the next sheet he wrote "Strategies and Tactics" at the top. These were things which supported the "Goals and Objectives," and included another long list of things he'd learned in his research meetings.

The Region had implemented an Employee Suggestion Program (ESP) to encourage line employees to identify and escalate ideas to reduce costs. And for every dollar of cost-savings which resulted from the suggestion, the employee received 25% of the first year's savings. This supported two goals which he'd already written down: improving profitability and enhancing employee morale and satisfaction. Once again, he had pages and pages of

"Strategies and Tactics" that he'd have to condense to a more succinct list.

Next he began developing a chart which he'd entitled "Challenges." He toyed with the idea of using another word: problems, inhibitors, obstacles, or something else – but felt that "Challenges" was a term which wouldn't be objectionable to the Regional GM or any of his staff that he included in the presentation scheduled for Friday. Again, his pages and pages of notes had many "challenges" facing the customer in the Spain and Portugal markets. Some of these not surprising – such as downward pressure on pricing due to competitors seeking to make inroads into these markets. Also, the rise of "Hyper-Markets" was giving these very large retailers more purchasing clout – further putting downward pressure on prices – and thus profits.

Curiously, he had learned that one of the challenges in Portugal was a cultural aversion to clear-colored carbonated beverages. He didn't understand precisely why, and was told that it was a long-standing historical difference among the Portuguese. Since a significant portion of the customer's revenues came from clear-colored carbonated beverages, this was obviously a "challenge" in Portugal! He knew it was a challenge that his product set couldn't address, but he noted it on the chart anyway to demonstrate his knowledge of the customer's markets and to enhance his credibility.

The next chart was the first time in the presentation that he would talk about his own company. He envisioned providing a little background regarding the long-term global relationship between the two firms. He also carefully reviewed the long list of "Challenges" he had documented. He knew it would be critical that he select challenges that he knew his company's product suite could address – indeed, had addressed – in other Regions around the world. But he knew that it was critical that this be done in a consultative fashion and couldn't be "salesy."

His objective was, on this chart, to present the products and solutions that addressed the customer's "challenges."

With unduly oversimplifying this process or making it appear easier than it is – and easy it is not – when the presenter presents the Agenda and asks the decision-making executive if it looks reasonable to him and he answers affirmatively, continuing this process throughout the presentation can only result in one logical or reasonable result: that there exists, at a minimum, a very real mutually beneficial opportunity in the two firms working together.

And as the presenter reviews the Goals, Objectives, Strategies and Tactics – which he knows have to be right – or very close to right because they came from the executive's own people, when he asks in a voice full of humility: "Is our understanding of the items on this chart, based on the research we've done, correct?", the worst thing that can happen is that the executive may suggest minor changes.

When the presenter moved on to the next chart, which were those challenges, problems, obstacles or inhibitors which were, frankly, making it difficult to accomplish those goals, objectives, strategies and tactics covered on the prior chart, he's just presented the sought-after "pain points."

After all of this discussion up to this point being entirely about the customer, the presenter said, "Now, I'd like to tell you a little bit about our company. As you can see from the bullets on this chart, our business is in working with organizations such as yours – confronting similar challenges – and helping them to overcome those challenges." And bullet-by-bullet, the points on the chart addressed each one of the issues presented on the prior chart.

"Now, sir, based on some of the challenges which your organization faces (which the executive has already agreed to), and the business we're in, does it seem like there is a very real potential benefit to our two firms working together?" This is when the presenter used his chart documenting the business-to-business alignment between both companies.

If done properly and in this order, how would any rational executive say "No?" And so the presenter quickly went to the last chart, which is the "Tell 'em what you told 'em chart." In short order, he reviewed what they'd covered that day, and on the very last bullet of this chart, the presenter said, "Based on our mutual agreement that it makes sense for us to work together, I've taken the liberty of suggesting some possible 'Next Steps.'"

And turning to the last chart, the executive saw something this, already "pre-filled:"

Action Item	Person Assigned	Due Date
Confirm "Business Fit"	AE	Today
Assign Project Manager (PM)	Exec	Today
Assign Team Members	PM	TBD
Develop Business Case	PM/AE	TBD
Implementation Plan	PM/AE	TBD
Monthly Progress Reviews	PM/AE/ Exec	TBD

Upon showing the chart, he put a check mark by the first item – indicating it had been completed. He then asked the executive if he had anyone in mind that may be an appropriate Project Manager. It's important to note that the presenter included "AE," for "Account Executive," to ensure that he personally was actively involved with the project to ensure it stayed on track. He also left the door open to meet with the executive on a monthly basis to "keep him abreast of how the project was going."

"You've done a very fine job today, sir. I'm particularly impressed that you accomplished all of this in the course of only one week. And I want you to know how much I appreciate you and your manager coming to Madrid to do this work – and I know that you sacrificed a holiday had you been in the States, and I appreciate that as well. Who do you think I should designate as the Project Manager?"

Somewhat taken aback, the Account Executive immediately suggested the "coach," Ramon, who had helped him with much of the work that was accomplished. The executive agreed, swiveled his chair to face Ramon and asked, "Ramon, are you up to this? It's a highly visible project."

Ramon responded, with a snappy "Yes sir," and the executive told him that he'd like to know the names of who Ramon would include on the team before the end of the next week.

Turning back to the Account Executive, the Regional President said, "Is there anything else you need from me?" The Account Executive responded, "Not at this time, sir."

"Good. Then get with my assistant and schedule the next four monthly Progress Reviews. If we don't get them on my calendar, they won't happen. Thanks again to both of you, and I wish you a safe journey home."

With that, he got up and left the room. As soon as the door shut behind him, "high fives" were flying among everyone left in the conference room. The week had been a success.

Chapter 11

Having demonstrated through using the principles of *Purposeful Selling*™ that there was a compelling alignment between the buying firm and the selling firm, another sales professional believed that the executive decision-maker would likely be inclined to agree to "do business." After all, he or she will have seen how the selling firm provides solutions which will 1) overcome the challenges confronting the buyer; 2) thereby enhancing the buyer's ability to implement his or her strategies and tactics; and 3) lead to the accomplishment of the buyer's goals and objectives.

But as we saw in the prior chapter, a key element of the last chart, the "Action Items," was the development of a compelling business case which met the customer's ROI and payback thresholds.

Proving that there's a "Business Fit" is a major step in developing the partnership, but almost any organization which will make a sizable investment has to meet certain internal thresholds – and it's the successful Sales Professional who ensures that this is "baked into" the Action Plan.

All of this is designed to motivate the buyer to make a decision in the seller's favor. And why not? What could be missing?

Purposeful Selling™ assumes that the buyer is making an investment. Consequently, to the extent that he could demonstrate a projection of the buyer's return on this investment (ROI), payback on this investment, or meet whatever financial threshold the buying organization uses to make a "go/no-go" decision on purchases, the more compelling the business case supporting the investment would be. More often than not, the principles practiced in this process will be used to justify the buyer's spending a significant amount of money – either a large capital investment or a large operating expense. It's critical that the sales professional "speak the language" of financial justification to support the sale. Or rather, the *investment*.

For the Sales Manager

Chapter 12

Because I came up the ranks through sales and marketing and as I reflect upon my career, I've been perhaps too tough on sales, marketing, and business professionals. I have high expectations of how each of us performs. I'm proud of the professions of selling and marketing and constantly want to see improvement. In much of what I do, I'm critical of what we do, how we act, how we perform. We should constantly be seeking to perform at the highest levels possible.

However, we are not alone in our responsibility and accountability to perform at the highest levels possible. Our direct managers are responsible and accountable for our performance, and leadership all the way up the food chain is accountable for assuring that the performance of each individual, team, and the organization as a whole is maximized.

Ultimately, performance and performance management is a question of leadership. It's the leader's responsibility to define what performance is in each role in the organization. It's the leader's responsibility to put people in those roles who have the skills, abilities, commitment, behaviors, and drive to perform as expected. It's the leader's responsibility to identify gaps in performance, helping the individual or organization to close those gaps. Whether through coaching, training, providing new processes, programs or tools, the job of the leader is to identify and close all performance gaps.

Sometimes, an individual, despite all the coaching, development and support, cannot or will not improve their performance to the point of meeting expectations. Clearly, they are in the wrong role and need to be moved into a role where they can perform – even if that means moving to another organization. It's a leader's responsibility to do this; not doing this is not the individual's fault, but the leader's fault. Having situations like this persist within an organization becomes the fault of senior leadership.

It's usually pretty easy to identify those people who cannot or will not perform to expectations. Too often, however, management fails to take timely action. Over time, performance will erode in the organization.

More often, however, I find great people with huge potential who have been badly managed. Their performance may not be at the desired level, but it is less their "fault" and more that of management (notice I am refraining from use of the word "Leader"). Too often, I find managers who simply don't care. They worry more about what's happening above them – "managing up – or pushing paper, than they do about their people. Or I find managers that have not defined performance expectations clearly, or they haven't coached or developed the people (or do a terrible job at it). I may find managers who are being badly managed themselves. In turn, the performance – or absence of performance – of these managers may not be addressed, and this is repeated all the way up the "food chain."

Too often we make mistakes with people. They may have performed badly and never improved because they were never coached, developed, or challenged and supported to perform better. These people, when "liberated" from a bad manager, can – and often do – thrive.

Put in the right job, understanding performance expectations, given the opportunity to perform, adequately coached and developed, they often become the best performers in the organization.

Consistent, sustained performance issues are never problems of the individual's; they are the problems of management and can go far up the food chain. We never "fix" consistent and sustained performance issues by addressing only the individual, but by looking at managers and what they are doing.

In fairness to managers, they may not understand it's their responsibility to manage performance. Too often they tend view their jobs as administrators. Or they may not have been trained, coached, or developed to serve as managers.

For the sales managers and executives who are reading this book, how do you define your job as a manager and leader? Are you working with your people or are you managing reports and pushing paper?

Somehow, over the years, "managing" was tagged as something negative, and only if one were a "leader" could success be defined.

For years, men's closets always had a brown suit. And if one could only have three suits, one was gray, one was dark blue and one was brown. But suddenly, the rules changed. When in 1975 John T. Molloy first published the landmark book, *Dress for Success*, sales of brown suits plummeted. And from this author's perspective, Molloy's single-handed "assassination" of the brown suit wasn't based on any quantitative or qualitative research. Rather, it seems that it was simply Molloy's opinion.

And similarly, while this author cannot pinpoint the date or event that "managing" received a similar assassination, the same fate indeed befell anyone who aspired to achieve excellence as a "manager." It's almost as though this group of people probably also wore brown suits! Being a "leader" became aspirational, not being a "manager."

Quite obviously, there's a place for both management <u>and</u> leadership for those who find themselves in a box on an organizational chart which has other boxes below it and connected to it. Aspiring for excellence in one doesn't discount the same aspiration for the other.

Generally speaking, it is the result of this author's "water-cooler-research" that leaders are associated with "firing up the troops." Managers, in this less-than-scientific research project, were associated with filling a role which is more "mechanical;" a sort of cog-in-the-wheel. But, these water-cooler research participants acknowledged that managers are the ones that "get things done." Without them, for example, the factory would probably shut down. The leader, on the other hand, would give the rank-and-file an inspiring and motivational "pep talk." And the "half-life," or "staying power," of this pep talk would be only a few hours. But clearly there are times when an inspiring, motivational "pep talk" can be of enormous benefit, particularly when morale is generally low for one reason or another.

So we don't see this as an "either/or" distinction. It is our view that the most effective executives are those who are able to blend elements of both a "manager" and a "leader."

In fact, we've developed a ten-point "checklist" of the elements which would go into this very effective "concoction" – or blend of manager and leader:

1. **Know Yourself**: Many people find this an unusual part of being an effective executive. But the effective executive is continually making a self-assessment of his or her weaknesses and seeking out opportunities to improve in these areas through reading, studying or continuing education.

2. **Be the Example**: People believe what they "see," not what they "hear." Be the role model. It's unrealistic to expect your team to "go the extra mile" when their executive is working a "9-to-5" workday. Model the

behavior that you want your team to exhibit.

3. **Be Responsible:** Take responsibility for your actions. Search for ways to guide your organization to new heights. And when things go wrong, do not blame others.

4. **Keep Your Team Informed:** The old adage, "knowledge is power," may be true. But that kind of power isn't what will allow you to accomplish things through others. Keep your team informed of good news and bad news.

5. **Over-communicate the Organization's Goals:** Share your vision at every opportunity – in group meetings and in one-on-one meetings. Ask for buy-in. When you get it, your vision becomes a shared vision and everyone is on the same page.

6. **Translate the Vision into Tasks:** Do this with your subordinates and make sure they do it with their subordinates. Ensure that the tasks are clearly understood, reviewed on a regular basis and accomplished. Measure and reward your people on their

accomplishment (or failure to accomplish) their tasks.

7. **Empower Your People:** Give them the tools they need to do their jobs and the latitude they need to accomplish their objectives. Develop a sense of accountability, ownership and responsibility in your people.

8. **Be Decisive:** Don't "sit on" decisions. Make them in a sound <u>and</u> timely basis. Use good problem solving, decision-making, and planning tools and let your people know how you arrived at your decision so that the process becomes a learning experience.

9. **Recognize Accomplishment and Failure:** "Praise in public, criticize in private" may be a cliché, but it's shocking how some leaders relish in humiliating their subordinates in public. Don't. But don't avoid confronting failure and turning that failure into a learning opportunity.

10. **Be Caring:** Know your people and look out for their well-being. Know human nature and the importance of sincerely caring for your workers. Send hand-written notes on

special occasions. If you know someone on your team has experienced a death in their family, don't be afraid to express your condolences. Better yet, attend the funeral. And if a family member of someone on your team graduates from college as a *Phi Beta Kappa*, send a note and share in their pride.

Quite clearly, it's not a question of whether the individual whose name is in the box on that organization chart -- with other boxes below it and connected to it -- is a "manager" or a "leader." He or she, to be most effective, has to be both.

Chapter 13

For purposes of this book, the author assumes a hierarchical organization structure. To be more specific, one person is the "boss" and the other answers to him or her. The boss – in this case – has the "power." But it's worth a review of the "Five Types of Power," as identified by John French and Bertram Raven in the 1960's.

French and Raven divided their five types of power into two distinct categories: formal power and personal power.

Formal Power

Coercive

Coercive power is conveyed through fear of losing one's job, being demoted, receiving a poor performance review, having prime projects taken away, etc. This power is gotten through threatening others. For example, the VP of Sales who threatens the sales team to meet their goals or get replaced.

Reward

Reward power is conveyed through rewarding individuals for compliance with one's wishes. This may be done through giving bonuses, raises, a promotion, extra time off from work, etc. One example is the supervisor who provides employees comp time when they meet a "stretch" objective she sets for a project.

Legitimate

Legitimate power comes from having a position of power in an organization, such as being the boss or a key member of a leadership team. This power comes when employees in the organization recognize the authority of the individual. For example, the CEO who determines the overall direction of the company and the corresponding resource needs.

Personal Power

Expert
Expert power comes from one's

experiences, skills or knowledge. As we gain experience in particular areas, and become thought leaders in those areas, we begin to gather expert power that can be utilized to get others to help us meet our goals. For example, the Project Manager who is an expert at solving particularly challenging problems to ensure a project stays on track exhibits expert power.

Referent

Referent power comes from being trusted and respected. We can gain referent power when others trust what we do and respect us for how we handle situations. For example, this may be the Human Resources Associate who is known for ensuring employees are treated fairly and who comes to the rescue of those who are not.

As we can see, one doesn't have to be in a leadership or senior level role in an organization to have some form of power. In fact, the most respect is garnered by those who have personal sources of power. There is more respect for these individuals than for those who have power simply because they are the boss in the business. It has been shown that when employees in an organization associate the leadership's power with expert or referent power, they are more engaged, more devoted to the organization and their role within it. Employees are also more willing to go the extra mile to reach organizational goals.

It's worth examining your own situation and asking the question: What is your source of power? And are you using the "right source" or simply throwing your weight around? How effectively do you use your source of power to meet key goals and objectives?

Sales Manager Profiles

<u>Chapter 14</u>

Exactly what is the role of the sales manager? Over the course of more than three decades in this profession, it's my view that Sales Managers fall into one of several categories; however, I am not suggesting that any one of these is the "right" answer or the "right" role for the sales manager.

1) <u>The Positive Reinforcer</u>. This is the manager who will hand out "attaboys" every time something goes well: from the forecast being accurate to displacing a competitor and winning over a customer "from the dark side." In addition to "attaboys," the sales manager is generous with bonuses and recognition before the sales professional's peers.

2) <u>Siskel and Ebert</u>. This manager is the critic and sees his or her role as to accompany the sales professional on customer calls, to take notes, and then provide feedback to the sales

professional on how he or she could have improved – curiously, this feedback on improvement usually begins with "...when I had a customer like this...I handled it this way..." After all, he or she wouldn't be a sales manager if it weren't for having excelled as a sales professional, right?

3) <u>Your new best friend</u>. Curiously, a significant number of sales managers want to be "liked." Nothing more. Nothing less. At first blush, this may seem surprising. But when one examines the myriad of studies regarding why people go into sales, one of the most often cited reasons is "recognition." According to www.thesaurus.com, what more is "recognition" than "acceptance, appreciation, remembering, respect, etc.?"

Sales managers get a wide variety of answers to the question, "Why would you want to be in Sales?" The money? That's the most preferred answer by Sales Managers, but there are others. You're in a position to help people solve their problems...if you can identify a "need" that your solution solves and that your customer has, you're a problem-solver – which can be satisfying. But far and away, the answer most sales managers want to hear is that you're "money-motivated." This author finds that answer a bit gauche, and it has never had any bearing on my career decisions.

Returning to the discussion regarding "manager" versus "leader," what about "coach?" The subject raises some interesting questions. For one, in sports it's almost a given that the coach won't be able to perform as well as the players. There are, of course, some exceptions – but by the time even Hall-of-Famers such as Bart Starr went into coaching, he was well past his prime and could never compete with his players. There may be exceptions, but they're precious few.

Most would agree that the issue is largely moot. The hope would be that a coach would be able to accomplish a "skills transfer" to the players, although even that goal is suspect. A coach who was a former player wouldn't be able to accomplish much of a "skills transfer," unless, of course, he was coaching a player in the same position that he played. That leaves the coach, or manager, with the not unimportant job of strategy, player development, recruiting and player evaluations -- and an occasional pep talk.

How does this "translate" in sales and the dynamics between the sales professional and the sales manager?

First, let's assume that the sales manager has embraced <u>some</u> methodology – and that it's been proven to work – at least for him or her. And by "embraced," we mean that the sales manager has internalized this methodology to the point of being a zealot. He or she is dogmatic in its use. And he or she <u>is</u> capable of accomplishing the necessary skills transfer from Sales Manager to Sales Professional to ensure a successful outcome.

In the next chapter, we'll get into the specifics of exactly what skills are to be transferred. And more to the point, how those skills will be transferred.

Why Buy From Me?

Chapter 15

Much has been made of "Consultative Selling" and other selling methodologies, such as "Relationship Selling," or "Value-Based Selling." Go to the Business Section of any library or bookstore, and there will be a plethora of books – all touting something "new" or "the latest" in selling methodology.

Selling's been around for a long time, and this author doesn't think that there's much "new" to learn. Having said that, for purposes of this book, let's say that there are two types of selling: "transactional selling" and "large account selling." Some will argue that there are more than two. Perhaps there are. But for the purposes of this book let's limit the types of selling to two, and by doing so we will limit ourselves to a "universe" of selling methodologies to what is, in essence, a binary choice.

And there are probably better labels, but that's just what they are – labels. So they'll do.

Now we'll add some definition to each, and again – these definitions are open to debate, but at some point the debating has to stop and we need to define our terms. Right or wrong, at least we'll be "speaking the same language." The author acknowledges that others may have different – and arguably, better – definitions, and that the limiting of the methodologies to two is arbitrary. There could be as many methodologies as there are opinions. That said:

• Transactional selling: this is selling which may have some or all of the following characteristics:

   ◦ Generally a "one-time-only" sale, i.e. not a lot of "repeat" business;

   ◦ The "average ticket" price is on the low end of the spectrum (and "low end" will vary depending upon who's defining it);

   ◦ Close attention must be paid to the "Cost of Selling." If the "Cost of Selling" is too high relative to the selling price, it's easy to see how this could quickly become an unprofitable business. This will change over time, and, in fact, can be observed. Those of us with enough gray hair can remember "The Fuller Brush Man" (and no sexism is intended – they were almost always men) knocking on our front door to sell his variety of brushes. The cost of doing business this way – relative to the profits associated with selling a few brushes – made "The Fuller Brush Man" go the way of the dinosaur.

- Large Account Selling: This is a type of selling which may have some or all of the following characteristics:

  ○ Large Account Selling could just as easily be referred to as "Repeat Business" selling. Previously, we described one of the characteristics of "Transactional Selling" as having an "average ticket" price on the low end of the spectrum. But, as with so many things, it's often the exception which brings the definition into relief for us. By way of example, consider the yellow, Number 2, wooden pencil. On average, the same pencil you used to take the ACT or the SAT as a precursor to attending college or university

sells for about 10¢ each.   Cost-adjusted for
inflation, this is actually less than you
probably paid for the one you used.

To sell these pencils door-to-door
would obviously be cost-prohibitive.   To sell
them to a roomful of students taking the SAT
or the ACT would probably even be cost
prohibitive.   But, if your customer is the
Superintendent of Schools who buys these
pencils for the entire school district – and who
probably places several orders during the
school year – we've crossed over from what was
transactional selling ("average ticket" price on
the low end of the spectrum) to what would
more likely be "large account" selling.

- Clearly, there would be
sufficient "repeat business" to be in the "large
account selling" category.
- While finance people are always
cognizant of the Cost   of Selling (and all
costs, for that matter), intuitively we believe that
the "Cost of Selling" isn't going to make this
product or this customer unprofitable.   Throw in
a few business lunches, a nice gift during the

holidays -- heck – throw in two tickets to the Super Bowl – it's just not likely that the cost of sales will make this product or this customer unprofitable given the sheer number of pencils they're going to purchase.

Now that we know we're dealing with Large Account Selling, some things become clear:

- We're probably likely to spend the time, effort and money to develop a "relationship" with the buyer (or buyers). As we'll see when dealing with large accounts, often there are <u>many</u> buyers. As we reviewed previously, there will be many people to whom we must sell simply because they have the power to say "no," even though they don't or won't have the authority to say "yes."

- Unlike in a transactional sale, we're likely to make an extensive effort to understand our customer's business. And by this, we mean understanding its goals and strategies, its tactics and objectives, and the challenges it faces (or what we may also refer to as obstacles, impediments, or problems – those things which are keeping it from accomplishing its tactics, objectives, goals and strategies).

- We're highly likely to determine the "value" associated with our product – or what we're more likely to refer to as our "solution." The <u>solution</u> is how we'll define what we're selling so as to avoid being considered a commodity – a trap which is essential that we avoid. It probably will consist of our service, out technological advantages, our support: essentially, anything to which we can assign a dollar value which either contributes to increased revenue or decreased costs.

- "Application" discovery. Again, to avoid the "commodity trap, we want to identify new applications for our yellow, #2 pencil which will contribute to its "uniqueness." For example, can we come out with a product variant in a different "form-factor?" That is, can we develop a version which is "dressier?" One with en elegant case and a clip which allows us to carry it in our breast pocket? And maybe one that's <u>not</u> erasable – except, of course, if the user is erasing what he or she has written using our newly-patented and cleverly-designed eraser which, to the unknowing observer, is covered by a removable cap. The cap, by way of example, is available in variations resembling college or university mascots – and the one which the account team will present to the Superintendent is, of course, <u>one with his or her mascot.</u>

It's important that we feel comfortable, particularly on a visceral level, that we've "covered our bases."

      ○   Have we developed a "personal relationship" with the ultimate decision maker? Do we know his or her spouse by name?

◦   And while our relationships may not be as deep, have we developed personal relationships with all of the other buyers – any of whom can say "No" to our solution?

◦   Have we demonstrated the uniqueness of our "solution" which ensures that it's not confused with those "commodities" offered by the other vendors?

Most companies recruit from colleges or universities in relatively close proximity to the location at which they'll work.   Have we considered a "mock up," or full-size cardboard cutout of a man or a woman wearing one of the elegantly-designed versions of the product with the mascot of one of those schools, that we can display in the lobby (or lobbies)?

◦   Have we developed, in a clearly defined fashion, the <u>value</u> of our solution? Can we show the increased profitability our solution will provide?   Do we have the agreement from one or more of the buyers to this number?

◦   Can we deliver an executive presentation which, by "reverse-engineering," shows how our solution contributes to the attainment of our customer's goals and objectives?

Lastly, we've not discussed our competitors. It's not because we don't have any – no matter the size of our account – there are others who want to displace us. Complacency can be a company's death-knell.

Andy Grove led Intel during a period when the company became the world's largest chip-maker and was also on everyone's list of "Most Admired Companies." In Grove's best-selling book – *Only the Paranoid Survive* - he describes the "nightmare moments" which led to his paranoia. The book should be on every executive's "must read" list.

Anyone who has read the book understands the risks of complacency which exist at almost every company. Our consulting firm uses a SWOT Analysis when working with our clients: Strengths, Weaknesses, Opportunities and Threats. Whether a leader chooses to use a SWOT Analysis or some other method of ensuring that its "eyes are wide open," the critical point is that it be done! And done regularly. And honestly. And thoroughly. And rigorously.

In most organizations, there exists a natural reluctance to be the one who delivers "bad news." One of the roles of the senior-most leaders of any organization is ensuring that no one "kills the messenger," and that the firm actively seeks out the risks, the exposures, and the threats it faces. How will the leaders know when they've gotten it right? They'll know when a paranoia – a healthy paranoia – permeates the organization. Not just at the senior leadership level but throughout the organization.

An Honorable Profession
Chapter 16

The reader may have noticed that the author rarely refers to "sales reps" or "sales people." These terms aren't necessarily bad. But for someone who's made a career out of selling, the term "Sales Professional" seems more fitting. Indeed, in many companies, the highest paid employee is not the President or the Chief Executive Officer, but the highest-performing sales professional! And, at least to this "old dog," that's as it should be.

I am aware of a circumstance in which the CEO of a leading consumer electronics retailer – whom I won't name, but their name suggests that at one time they sold a lot of "radios" – did exactly that. And had that top-performing sales professional been, quite coincidentally, a personal friend – I'm not sure I'd have believed it.

I find it interesting that if one were to survey incoming freshman at any college or university and asked, "What do you want to do when you graduate?", few would answer: I want to go into sales! Most would say they hope to be a doctor, lawyer, dentist, veterinarian, engineer, architect, accountant – ANYTHING but a sales professional! And yet, my own experience is that with the benefit of hindsight, many of those folks who began college with those careers in mind – and even many of those who achieved those goals – a great number would end up in sales.

All of my own roommates in college majored in Engineering – a particularly rigorous academic program at my *alma mater* – and I remember well their working until the wee hours of the morning studying such arcane subjects as "statics" or "dynamics" or "fluid mechanics." I confess that I had no idea (nor interest) in what these subjects even were!

But I chose to major in Marketing within the College of Business Administration. And while there were certainly courses that tested me and challenged me, it prepared me well for a career in sales.

To this day, I bristle when I hear someone refer to his or her title as "Account Manager," or "Account Executive," or "Business Development Executive." Early in my career at IBM, there was an almost-legendary executive whose name was Buck Rodgers. Really. That was his name. Well, actually it was Francis G. Rodgers. But everyone knew this legend as "Buck." And Rodgers looked like he was straight out of Central Casting as the quintessential business executive. In fact, in a book about the "Ten Greatest Salespeople," Rodgers was one of those cited. But even Rodgers couldn't force himself to refer to members of the IBM sales force as Sales Representatives. No. They were "Marketing Representatives." And thus I began my sales career as a Marketing Representative at IBM.

I confess that it was a bit difficult to explain my title to friends and colleagues who were "really" in marketing, but worse than that was that none other than Buck Rodgers couldn't bear to refer to his sales team with titles that reflected their profession.

And sales is an honorable profession. And most of the clichés associated with it are just that: cliché. The sales professionals with whom I've worked, in the main, are ethical, hard-working, bright, creative and active contributors to society through community groups, volunteer agencies and other activities. In short, they're just like any other "professional."

Indeed, today's sales professional who is responsible for one of his or her company's largest customers has a job that is absolutely critical to his company's success. To be successful in this role, he or she must consider their role as a "consultant" to his customer. While this term is used too liberally in my view, it should be the aspirational goal of every Major Account Sales Professional. The greatest compliment a customer can give his or her Sales Professional is that they are viewed as

"Trusted Advisors" to the customer's organization.

This accomplishment does not happen overnight and takes a real and sustained commitment to learn the customer's business: its goals, objectives, strategies, tactics and its challenges, obstacles, problems and inhibitors. Upon <u>truly</u> learning the customer's business, only then can the sales professional offer solutions to his or her customer's challenges. And the very best – the truly elite of the Major Account Sales Professionals – will not only uncover a problem and deliver a solution. He or she will summon from their well of creative energy new and breakthrough innovations which will propel his or her customer past its competitors and open up new sources or revenues and profits. But it can't happen without making the commitment to "walk in the customer's shoes."

Too often, it's my observation that those who fit the mold I've described get promoted, get transferred or join another company before truly recognizing their potential with the large account to which they've been assigned. Corporate America has yet to build a "career path" for those whose gifting and passion is selling. Instead, they get promoted to management – and it's often been said – with a great deal of truth – that a good sales <u>professional</u> doesn't necessarily make a good sales <u>manager</u>. So why don't companies develop a parallel track for these talented professionals? Why does the sales professional have to be "promoted" to earn more money or to get a bigger office or to benefit from the perks that come with being a manager?

When I was approaching my college graduation, it was my good fortune to be presented with several job opportunities. My question for each company was always the same: "How high can I go in your company if I begin in sales?" More often than not, the answer was along the lines of "Vice President of Sales." But IBM was different. At that time, every Chairman, every President, and every Chief Executive Officer in the history of

IBM had begun his career in sales. So my decision was easy.

I then had the opportunity to join the Hewlett-Packard Company. By any measure, H-P is a company to be admired. Bill Hewlett and Dave Packard were the original entrepreneurs who created what we know now as Silicon Valley. The company treated its employees well, made great products, demonstrated a culture of innovation and was widely admired around the world. I stayed for less than two years, despite achieving over 400% of my quota and making more money than I ever had in my career. But H-P viewed the sales organization as "the channel." One of many if other channel partners are included. In fact, I happened to join the firm in Los Angeles. Now, for any other company, that would be the Western Region. But not at H-P. At H-P, it was the "Neely Region." Why? Because Norm Neely was the original manufacturer's rep – "the channel" – when H-P first started doing business in the Western United States. While I was there, an announcement was made about an IBM executive who had come up through the sales ranks and was promoted to run a large, multi-national engineering and manufacturing organization which produced products that accounted for over $5 billion of IBM's revenues. Coincidentally, the executive had worked in the same branch sales office that I did, and while not close, I knew him personally -- having worked in the same office. Sharing this news with my peers at H-P generated some of the most quizzical looks I've ever seen in my professional career! A salesman running a multi-billion dollar engineering and manufacturing organization? Why, that was heresy at a company renowned for its engineering excellence! It was simply inconceivable that someone whose background was in sales could be in such a position. "Never at H-P," was the proud refrain.

Do not misunderstand the message I am attempting to convey. Cream rises to the top, regardless of whether the "cream" begins his or her career in sales, marketing, operations, finance, engineering, manufacturing or any other discipline. There is absolutely no reason that a gifted engineering professional can't also ascend to run a global sales organization. And I'm sure many have. My point is simply this: it is my hope that any organization will not limit the career of the talented sales professional. It is my hope that companies will develop career paths for sales professionals which truly parallel those who choose to move into management. It is my hope that surveys of incoming college freshman about their career aspirations will indicate that many aspire to be "sales professionals." It is my hope that the stereotypes and clichés associated with sales professionals will melt away like snow in the spring. It is my hope that the sales professional will not feel the least bit sheepish when asked at a cocktail party what he or she does for a living.

Lastly, it is my hope that the sales professional will accept the responsibility for continuing his or her professional development. For honing his or her craft. For achieving the status of "Trusted Advisor" to his or her customer. For not only solving his or her customer's problems, but in "leading" the customer in the application of his or her products, services or solutions to deliver "breakthrough innovation" which jettisons the customer into a position of sustainable competitive advantage. But it is incumbent on us – those of us who make our careers in the profession of selling – to reach out and take this gauntlet. The best of the best will do so. And they will reap the rewards – and not just the monetary rewards – but the rewards that come from extraordinary accomplishment and which will result in an "inner" feeling of a quiet pride that we are privileged to be able to make sales our profession.

About the Author

George Devitt has spent more than three decades in roles which have included sales and sales management. A student of the profession and of those who have chosen to make a career of selling, Devitt has applied his unique skills of observation to assessing what works and what doesn't work in sales and selling. And his conclusion is that, as with any profession, a measurable and demonstrable improvement in performance will result from a serious commitment to continuing professional development and the ongoing development of the skills required for success in the sales profession.

It is Devitt's firm conviction and his foundational principle, not shared by many inside or outside of his field, that there is no such thing as "a born salesman," just as there is no such thing as "a born lawyer" or "a born dentist" or "a born automobile mechanic." Rather, each profession has a skill-set with which it is associated that can be both grown (new skills learned) and refined (existing skills honed).

And, as with any profession, continuing and ongoing professional development should be undertaken so that the sales professional can hone his skills and master her craft.

Devitt has made a career of observing and documenting the traits and skills of the successful sales professional and incorporating those observations into professional development programs to improve and refine the skills of the sales professional so that, over time, the likelihood of success in his or her chosen profession increases.

Unlike continuing professional development in most fields, meetings of sales professionals are largely devoted to motivational programs intended to "rally the troops" and heighten the enthusiasm of the sales organization. While enjoyable enough, the investment in these programs has a very short "half-life." Devitt's assertion is that by the time the sales professional has returned to his or her home office after a motivational sales meeting, the enthusiasm has largely worn off and the sales professional is left with, at best, an 8" x 10" framed picture of himself shaking hands with Dan Marino, the keynote speaker, while the company's Vice President of Sales looks on with a broad smile. While a motivational program, with its short half-life, may have the intended effect for the football team about to take the field at the beginning of a game, there is a large chasm between the sixty minutes that it takes to complete the football game and the twelve months it takes the sales professional to achieve his or her annual quota.

Purposeful Selling isn't an event. It's a process. And done properly, its benefits will endure long after any "motivational event" or one-time workshop. I use it myself, I use it in conducting sales training and development with my clients and I've seen it done by others. I've even witnessed one CEO try to <u>hire</u> the sales professional on-the-spot after she'd completed the presentation! Does it work? You bet it does!

www.ingramcontent.com/pod-product-compliance
Lightning Source LLC
Chambersburg PA
CBHW081309170526
45166CB00011B/3464